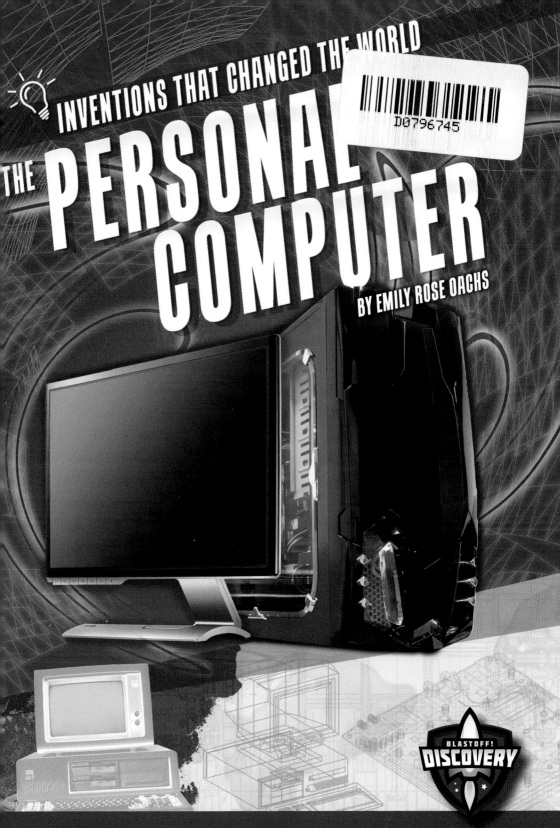

INVENTIONS THAT CHANGED THE WORLD

THE PERSONAL COMPUTER

BY EMILY ROSE OACHS

D0796745

Bellwether Media • Minneapolis, MN

Blastoff! Discovery launches a new mission: reading to learn. Filled with facts and features, each book offers you an exciting new world to explore!

This edition first published in 2019 by Bellwether Media, Inc.

No part of this publication may be reproduced in whole or in part without written permission of the publisher.
For information regarding permission, write to Bellwether Media, Inc., Attention: Permissions Department,
6012 Blue Circle Dr., Minnetonka, MN 55343.

Library of Congress Cataloging-in-Publication Data

Names: Oachs, Emily Rose, author.
Title: The Personal Computer / by Emily Rose Oachs.
Description: Minneapolis, MN : Bellwether Media, Inc., 2019.
  | Series: Blastoff! Discovery. Inventions that Changed the
  World | Includes bibliographical references and index. |
  Audience: Ages 7-13.
Identifiers: LCCN 2018040246 (print) | LCCN 2018042130
  (ebook) | ISBN 9781681037035 (ebook) | ISBN
  9781626179691 (hardcover : alk. paper) | ISBN
  9781618915122 (pbk. : alk. paper)
Subjects: LCSH: Electronic digital computers–History–Juvenile
  literature.Classification: LCC QA76.23 (ebook) | LCC
  QA76.23 .O233 2019 (print) | DDC 004–dc23
LC record available at https://lccn.loc.gov/2018040246

Editor: Betsy Rathburn   Designer: Josh Brink

Printed in the United States of America, North Mankato, MN

TABLE OF CONTENTS

HOMEWORK HELPER

A student gets home from school. He sits down at the computer. Then, he presses the machine's power button and waits for the computer to boot up. He has a report to write about the nation's capital.

When the computer turns on, the boy opens a music program. With a click, a soft tune starts to play. Next, the boy pulls up a blank document and opens a web **browser**. He is ready to begin researching.

The boy reads through articles about the capital. He finds some sketches of the buildings from when they were first built. Then, he watches some videos showing major landmarks. As the boy researches, he takes notes.

The boy's parents call him to dinner. He stretches and yawns as he rises from the computer. He will come back to start writing later. With the personal computer, all he needs to write his report is right in front of him!

ROOM-SIZED TO DESK-SIZED

The earliest computing devices date back centuries. Simple devices such as the **abacus** were designed to do math problems. The first **mechanical** computers were designed in the 1800s. Among the first was Charles Babbage's Analytical Engine. Though it was not built in his lifetime, its design influenced all future computers.

abacus

DID YOU KNOW?

ENIAC was a giant machine. It was made up of 18,000 vacuum tubes and 6,000 switches. It weighed 60,000 pounds (27,216 kilograms)!

ENIAC

The first modern electric computer came in 1946. Like other early computers, ENIAC was programmed only to do specific calculations. **Vacuum tubes** made up ENIAC's **central processing unit** (CPU). The tubes made the computer so big that it took up an entire room!

9

Major advances came in 1971 with the first **microprocessor**. This small device gave computers more power while also making them smaller and cheaper. A few years later, the Altair 8800 was released. Many consider it the first personal computer!

Altair 8800

ALTAIR DISK

ALTAIR 8800 COMPUTER

DID YOU KNOW?

The 1975 Altair 8800 came as a kit. Users had to build it themselves. There was no keyboard or screen. Switches and lights were used to enter and retrieve information!

Commodore PET

In 1977, Apple released the Apple II personal computer. That same year, the TRS-80 and Commodore PET were released. Each computer had a screen and built-in keyboard. They helped launch a personal computer boom. By 2017, there were more than one billion personal computers around the world!

POWERING UP

The Apple II helped shape future personal computers. It came with a sleek design, color **graphics**, and room for more **memory**. Apple II was also the first computer to run a **spreadsheet** program. The program, VisiCalc, quickly became popular among businesses. It placed the Apple II in even higher demand.

Apple II

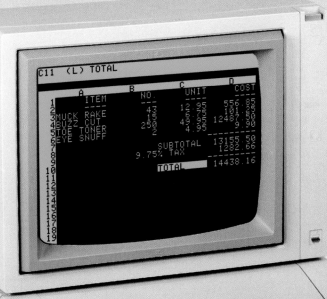

VisiCalc software

```
C11 (L) TOTAL
           A    ITEM       B   NO.    C  UNIT        D    COST
 1
 2                              43      12.95          556.85
 3  MUCK RAKE                   15       6.75          101.95
 4  BUZZ CUT                   250      49.95        12487.50
 5  TOE TONER                    2       4.95            9.90
 6  EYE SNUFF
 7                              SUBTOTAL            13155.50
 8              9.75% TAX                            1282.66
 9
10                             TOTAL                14438.16
11
12
13
14
15
16
17
18
19
```

VisiCalc's popularity helped show how **software** expanded the uses of computers. Soon, developers were creating new spreadsheet programs, **word processors**, and even games. These programs made computers functional and fun!

More change came in 1981 with the IBM 5150. At the computer's heart was the **motherboard**, which stored **RAM**. It ran Microsoft's PC-DOS **operating system**. IBM made the computer's design public. Other developers made products to work with the computer.

More advances led to even more modern computers. In 1983, Apple's Lisa personal computer was among the first to use a **graphical user interface** (GUI). Users no longer had to type in commands to run programs. Instead, they used a mouse to click icons and send the computer instructions. This system is still used today!

Apple Lisa

HOW IT WORKS

PERSONAL COMPUTER

1   2   3

1. Input:

The user sends commands to the computer by typing on the keyboard or clicking with the mouse.

2. Processing:

The motherboard completes the operation, using the computer's RAM and other storage to make the process faster.

3. Output:

The command requested appears on the screen.

DID YOU KNOW?

In 1964, David Engelbart and Bill English created the first-ever computer mouse. It took 20 years for the mouse to become commonly used!

As computers became more advanced, users wanted to be able to travel more easily with them. This sparked a wave of portable computers in the early 1980s. The 1981 Osborne 1 was the first successful portable computer. This 24-pound (11-kilogram) computer folded up into its plastic case. It had a handle for easier carrying.

The first true laptop was released the following year. Epson's briefcase-sized HX-20 came with a word processor and a built-in printer. The success of these early laptops paved the way for future portable personal computers!

Osborne 1

STEVE WOZNIAK

Born:	August 11, 1950, in San Jose, California
Background:	Inventor who co-founded Apple, Inc. in 1975 after studying math, science, and computers
Invented:	Apple II
Year Invented:	1977
Idea Development:	After the success of the Apple I, Wozniak worked with Steve Jobs to create an even better computer. They used their earnings to develop Apple's first computer meant for home use. It brought games, word processors, and spreadsheets to homes across the country!

An even greater burst in personal computer popularity came in the 1990s. The Internet started as a government project for scientists. But in 1991, the **World Wide Web** gave anyone with a computer access to the **network**.

As more people logged onto the Internet, computers continued to shrink in size. By the mid-1990s, many personal computers were pocket-sized. This trend continued into the 2000s. By 2007, the Apple iPhone was released. Smartphones like the iPhone have many of the same functions as personal computers.

DID YOU KNOW?

In 1969, NASA's Apollo mission sent the first humans to the moon. Four computers helped them get there. Just one of today's smartphones holds more power than those computers!

THE DIGITAL AGE

After 35 years, personal computers have become central to many people's daily lives. They are found nearly everywhere! Millions of Americans use personal computers when they go to work each day. Most have a desktop or laptop computer at home as well. More than three out of four carry smartphones with them.

desktop

laptop

Personal computers brought big changes to many jobs. Engineers began using computers to create plans for bridges and buildings. Editing films became much easier. Some workers lost their jobs to computers. Computers could finish the work faster than they could.

Daily tasks were also simplified thanks to personal computers. People could more easily track schedules, create budgets, and store photos. It even became possible to order clothing, food, and other goods with the click of a button!

Personal computers make entertainment more accessible. With music players, people store thousands of albums on a single device. E-readers can hold more digital books than an actual bookshelf! Users may watch movies and television shows whenever they desire!

e-reader

DID YOU KNOW?

New types of jobs rose from the personal computer. Companies dedicated to software programming sprang up. Offices even hired workers just to help other workers with computer problems!

APPLE MACBOOK

Inventor's Name: Apple, Inc.

Year of Release: May 2006

Uses: Apple's original MacBook had a stylish yet powerful design. It could access the Internet, store music and images, and run many programs. It featured a full keyboard, a 13.3-inch (33-centimeter) screen, and a built-in webcam. Later models added even more features!

Personal computers allow instant communication between distant places. It takes days for a letter to arrive in the mail. But it takes only a few seconds for an e-mail to reach someone!

DID YOU KNOW?

In 1993, there were 130 web sites on the Internet. By 2017, that number had risen to almost 1.8 billion!

Social media has brought faster communication, too. It lets users share messages and photos with their networks. They can create friendships with people they might never meet in person. The personal computer brings the world to people's fingertips!

A NEW WAY

Tech companies have big plans for future computers. Some hope to create personal computers with few or no wires. Others are working to improve wearable technology, such as smart glasses or smart watches. Still others are designing computers so tiny that they can be inserted into a person's body!

smart glasses

Companies are also developing
3D **sensors** for their future computers.
These pick up on users' sounds and
hand movements to control the
computer. Decades after the first
computer mouse, new advances may
change the way people interact with
the computer all over again!

PERSONAL COMPUTER TIMELINE

1946

ENIAC becomes the first modern electric computer

1971

Intel builds its first microprocessor

1969

ARPAnet, which later becomes the Internet, is created

1974

The Altair 8800 computer kit becomes available

1981

Microsoft's PC-DOS operating system is introduced in the IBM 5150

1983

Apple's Lisa uses a graphical user interface and a mouse

2007

Apple introduces its first smartphone, the iPhone

1977

The Apple II, TRS-80, and Commodore PET personal computers go on the market

1991

The World Wide Web is released to the public

2019-

Future developments

GLOSSARY

abacus—a frame with rows of wires along which beads are moved; an abacus is used for calculating math problems.

browser—a program used to access the World Wide Web

central processing unit—the part of the computer that processes data

graphical user interface—a computer system that allows a user to control a computer by clicking icons and windows using a mouse

graphics—images on a computer screen

mechanical—made or operated using parts such as levers and gears instead of electronic parts

memory—the part of the computer that stores information

microprocessor—a chip that holds a computer's CPU

motherboard—the circuit board that holds a personal computer's CPU, memory, and other key parts

network—a group of connected objects that operate together

operating system—computer software that allows programs to run

RAM—random access memory; RAM is a type of computer memory that is used to run programs.

sensors—devices that can pick up on movement and sounds

software—the programs a computer runs

spreadsheet—a computer program that allows users to run calculations

vacuum tubes—tubes with no air that allow electricity to pass through

word processors—computer programs that allow users to create and store text

World Wide Web—a part of the Internet where users click links to move from page to page

TO LEARN MORE

AT THE LIBRARY

Beevor, Lucy. *The Invention of the Computer*. Mankato, Minn.: Capstone Press, 2018.

Doeden, Matt. *Steve Jobs: Technology Innovator and Apple Genius*. Minneapolis, Minn.: Lerner Publications, 2017.

Green, Sara. *Bill Gates*. Minneapolis, Minn.: Bellwether Media, 2015.

ON THE WEB

FACTSURFER

Factsurfer.com gives you a safe, fun way to find more information.

1. Go to www.factsurfer.com.

2. Enter "personal computer" into the search box.

3. Click the "Surf" button and select your book cover to see a list of related web sites.

INDEX